HEROES AND WARRIORS

FIONN MAC CUMHAIL

CHAMPION OF IRELAND

JOHN MATTHEWS

Plates by JAMES FIELD

Firebird Books

For Emrys

Acknowledgements

Special thanks must go to my wife Caitlín, who took time out from her own work to help me with typing, advised me on details of clothing and obscure points of Irish social history, and generally supported me through many hair-tearing sessions. Also to Rosemary Sutcliff, who generously allowed me to use whatever I needed from her own excellent retelling of the Fionn saga. Nor should one forget the great scholars who paved the way for this book – needless to say the errors are mine and not theirs. Finally (though by no means least), thanks again to Chesca Potter for her detailed work on the archaeological reconstructions used throughout the book.

J.M.

First published in the UK 1988 by Firebird Books

Copyright © 1988 Firebird Books Ltd, P.O. Box 327, Poole, Dorset BH15 2 RG
Text copyright © 1988 John Matthews

Distributed in the United States by
Sterling Publishing Co, Inc,
2 Park Avenue, New York, NY 10016

Distributed in Australia by
Capricorn Link (Australia) Pty Ltd
PO Box 665, Lane Cove, NSW 2066

British Library Cataloguing in Publication Data

Matthews, John, *1948–*
   Fionn Mac Cumhail : champion of Ireland.
   ——(Heroes and warriors series).
   1. Fionn Mac Cumhail (Legendary character)   2. Legends, Irish
   I. Title   II. Series
   398′.352   GR153.5

ISBN 1 85314 001 5

Series editor Stuart Booth
Designed by Kathryn S.A. Booth
Typeset by Colset Private Limited, Singapore
Colour separations by Kingfisher Facsimile
Colour printed by Butler and Tanner, Frome and London
Printed in Great Britain by Richard Clay Ltd, Chichester, Sussex

FIONN MAC CUMHAIL

CHAMPION OF IRELAND

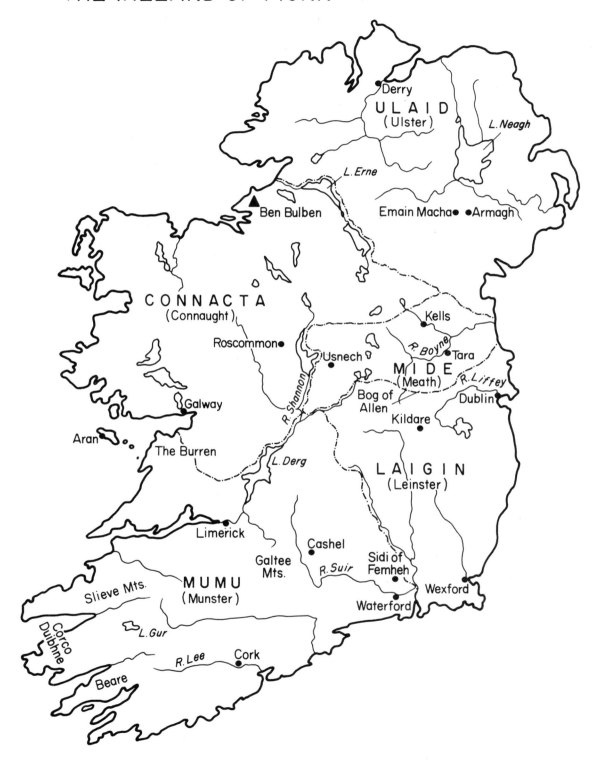

THE IRELAND OF FIONN

ULAID
(Ulster)

Derry

L. Neagh

L. Erne

Ben Bulben

Emain Macha • Armagh

CONNACTA
(Connaught)

Kells

R. Boyne

Roscommon •

Usnech

Tara

MIDE
(Meath)

R. Liffey

Galway

R. Shannon

Bog of
Allen

Dublin

Aran

Kildare

The Burren

L. Derg

LAIGIN
(Leinster)

Limerick

Cashel

Sidi of
Femheh

Wexford

Galtee
Mts.

R. Suir

Slieve Mts.

MUMU
(Munster)

Waterford

Corco
Duibhne

L. Gur

R. Lee

Cork

Beare

Long, long ago, beyond the misty space
Of twice a thousand years,
In Erin old there lived a might race
Taller than Roman spears.

Standish O'Grady

The Figure of Fionn

In Ireland, as well as in parts of Scotland today, people still speak of the hero Fionn mac Cumhail (Finn MacCool) as though his adventures had taken place only a few generations ago. Strange and wondrous tales are told of him: how, with his fearsome band of followers, the Fianna, he built the Giant's Causeway in a night; how he married a Faery Woman; and how he came to taste the flesh of the Salmon of Wisdom, from which he knew all things that were and had been and were yet to be. Others see him as a great and noble-hearted warrior of Ireland, whose deeds are recorded in the very substance of the land.

For the reality behind these tales, we have to turn to Ireland in the second and third centuries A.D., when the fierce and colourful Gaelic warriors lived, quarrelled and fought amid the hills and valleys and mountains. There Fionn, the warrior, chieftain, poet and seer saw his strange beginning; there gods and goddesses, the people of the *sidhe*, mingled with human men and women, and the border between the real world and the twilight realm of Faery was narrow and uncertain. In such times, you might meet an old woman on the road and only discover later that she was a goddess who held the sovereignty of the land as her lawful gift. Or the deer you were chasing might suddenly turn into a beautiful woman (as in the case of Fionn's wife Sadbh) only to vanish again, years later, as suddenly and unexpectedly as she had come.

In this world and in a time that was timeless, heroes like Fionn, or his son Oisin, or his grandson Oscar, or Cuchulainn, the 'Hound of Ulster', all moved in a twilight realm that was neither wholly real nor wholly imaginary. Questions of origin and historical status are still hotly debated. Yet beyond a certain point, an impenetrable wall is met with: history merges with myth and folk-lore, and the once bright figures become shadowy beings again.

Of Fionn himself, we have the following description, written down some 1,000 years after he may actually have lived, but still vibrant with the presence of a man who was as real to the writer as his own kith and kin.

And as to Finn himself, he was a king and a seer and a poet; a Druid and a knowledgeable man; and everything he said was sweet-sounding to his people. And a better fighting man than Finn never struck his hand into a king's hand, and whatever anyone ever said of him, he was three times better. And of his justice it used to be said, that if his enemy and his own son had come before him to be judged, it is a fair judgement he would have given between them.

5

And as to his generosity it used to be said, he never denied any man as long as he had mouth to eat with, and legs to bring away what he gave him; and he left no woman without her bride-price, and no man without his pay; and he never promised at night what he would not fulfil on the morrow, and he never promised in the day what he would not fulfil at night, and he never forsook his right-hand friend. And if he was quiet in peace he was angry in battle, and Oisin his son and Oscar his son's son followed him in that.

(trans: Lady Gregory)

History or Myth?

Contention still rages over the historicity of Fionn and the Fianna. Some hold them to be entirely mythical, a product of oral tradition and folk-lore; others say that Fionn was the historical captain of the warriors of King Cormac mac Art, High King of Ireland from 227–266 A.D.

According to the Annals of Ancient Ireland – written, it is true, long after the events they describe – Cumhail, Fionn's father, was the uncle of an earlier High King, Conn of the Hundred Battles. Conn's death is placed in the year 157, while Fionn's death is said to take place in 283 A.D., although the Battle of Gabhra, where he fell, is ascribed to a year later. These dates are close enough, and form a pattern sufficiently similar to establish a probable span for Fionn's life of the years 224–283 A.D., making him in his sixties at the time of his death and placing him firmly during the reign of Cormac.

The Fianna (Fionn's men), were a highly mobile, national militia, recruited from the war bands of the many local chieftains and Kings of Ireland – all serving, nominally, under the aegis of the High King at Tara. There seem to have been seven such bands, each consisting of some 3,000 men and a commander. Fionn, like his father Cumhail, began by commanding the men of Leinster and Meath – specifically the clan Bascna – but came in time to be captain of the whole Fianna, more than 20,000 men.

Their task was to protect Ireland's coastline from invasion, and to help keep the King's law or as the Annals of Clonmacnoise express it 'to uphold justice and to prevent injustice', as well as 'putting a stop to robbery, exacting the payment of tribute, putting down malefactors'. To do this successfully they were placed, in certain instances, outside the law, so that even their kin were unable to claim compensation in the event of the death of any one of the Fianna while on active service.

The setting up of this elite core of warriors is placed at the door of the King, Cormac mac Art, who is described as Ireland's first law-maker, and as conqueror of Alba (Scotland) and of most of Ireland itself. In the words of the unbiased chronicler of Clonmacnoise, he was:

Absolutely the best king that ever reigned in Ireland before himself . . . wise, learned, valiant and mild, not given causelessly to be bloody as many of his ancestors were; he reigned majestically and magnificently.

(trans: C. Mageoghagan)

6

None of this can be proved historically. Nevertheless, scholars have tended to accept it as probable, if not provable. Documents relating to the period are non-existent, and the later accounts, written down by monkish scribes hundreds of years later, are often inaccurate and contradictory.

The image which we derive from a reading of the cycles of stories relating to Fionn and Cormac may themselves be wide of the mark. That there was a High King in Tara may well have been recognised by all; but there were many who would not have acknowledged him or his right to command them, or to draw upon them to furnish men and arms for the Fianna.

A very similar situation existed in Britain some 300 years later, when fear of the invading Saxons caused the scattered and quarrelsome chieftains to band together under a leader who was neither a king nor owed allegiance to any one master. He too, like Fionn, commanded a band of dedicated soldiers, drawn from many areas of the country and also mobile by reason of their equestrian status.

The Giant's Causeway in Co. Antrim is said to have been built in one day by the 'giant' Fionn when he became tired of getting wet feet everytime he crossed to Scotland to steal cattle. This stems from a much later idea of the figure of Fionn.

7

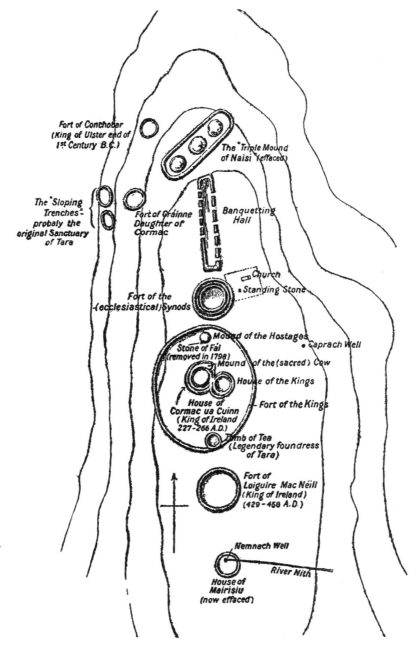

Fort of Conchobar
(King of Ulster end of
1st Century B.C.)

The "Triple Mound
of Naisi (effaced)

The "Sloping
Trenches"
probaly the
original Sanctuary
of Tara

Fort of Gráinne
Daughter of
Cormac

Banquetting
Hall

Church

Standing Stone

Fort of the
(ecclesiastical) Synods

Mound of the Hostages

Caprach Well

Stone of Fál
(removed in 1798)

Mound of the (sacred) Cow

House of the Kings

House of
Cormac ua Cuinn
(King of Ireland
227-266 A.D.)

Fort of the Kings

Tomb of Tea
(Legendary foundress
of Tara)

Fort of
Loiguire Mac Néill
(King of Ireland)
(429 - 458 A.D.)

Nemnach Well

River Nith

House of
Mairisiu
(now effaced)

The principle sites of the Hill of Tara (after R.A.S. Macallister). Tara was the place of Kings for many generations before and after the Fianna, as the many archaeological remains still testify.

This man was Arthur, who like Fionn became mythologised into the towering figure of King Arthur, surrounded by his glittering Knights of the Round Table. With Arthur, it is clear that we are dealing with the memory of a remarkable man, whose legendary stature is a measure of his human qualities. Similarly, in the case of Fionn, there may well have been a real character, whose unique abilities enabled him to hold together a band of warriors from the many tribes, and then to command such loyalty from them that they became an unequalled force in the land.

The King-mound at Tara. Here all of Ireland's high kings were installed, including Cormac mac Art, whom Fionn and the Fianna served.

Certainly, there is a roughness and humanity about the Fianna which make them far more believable than most heroes. Their stories take place in the open air, unlike the later Arthurian material which is more courtly in its setting. The Fianna's favourite pursuits were hunting, fighting and making love, and as we shall see in the stories retold later, they were not above placing personal safety above unnecessary heroics – despite their immense personal bravery. Fionn himself appeared so unwaveringly honest that he was often in trouble because of it: once he had given his word, we are told over and over again that 'he could not refuse' – not even if it meant, as it often did, putting himself and his men at great risk.

As with Arthur, we may never know the truth about Fionn. The best that can be said is that archaeological evidence points to a resurgence and consolidation in Ireland during the period of Cormac's reign. Also, we know that the attempts on the part of the Roman armies in Britain to infiltrate the Celtic kingdom across the narrow seas met with significant lack of success. Perhaps the numerous battles of Fionn against 'the King of the World' may recall his powerful repulsion of the most powerful fighting force then in existence.

Fionn's Ireland: third century A.D.

The Fionn cycle takes place in two worlds: that of the real Ireland and that of the otherworld, Tir-nan-Og or Tir-fa-Thon, the dwelling of the Lordly Ones. Between these two worlds, the free-ranging Fianna passed at will, their adventures taking them to and fro across the boundary of the unseen world at any time.

The reality of third century Ireland was a wild untamed land of forest, hill and marshland, teaming with game, birdlife and fish that stocked the rivers to bursting.

The people who lived there were farmers, Celts who had migrated from Europe almost a thousand years before. They kept cattle, pigs and goats, tilled the land and knew the arts of milling and weaving. They dressed in simple clothes dyed with bright colours, bathed frequently and cared about their appearance. They were a proud and warlike people, as their stories show, and they loved nothing better than to band together to raid their neighbours' lands for cattle and slaves. One of the most famous wars in their history began with such an event – the Cattle Raid of Cuailgne (Cooley) – in which Queen Medb (Maeve) of Connaught stole a famous bull from the lands of the Ulstermen and precipitated a conflict which involved Ireland's first great hero, Cuchulainn, and ended in his death.

The cow was, indeed, the basis of Ireland's economy until the eighth century, which finally saw the introduction of a coinage. By this standard, a cow was worth about an ounce of gold. Previously the measure was one cow to three slaves, usually female since these were believed to work harder and to be less likely to run away. The word for a female bondslave was *cumhal*, which caused at least one writer to assume that Fionn was the son of a slave! Burglary was virtually unknown, most local crime being based on the theft of cattle. After all, cattle could make a poor man rich overnight if he had the strength of arm to keep what he had acquired.

When they were not fighting, raiding or hunting, the people of Fionn's day lived in isolated farmsteads called forts – though these were not always intended for military use or defence. Circular, between 130 and 160 feet in diameter, they consisted of a flattened area surrounded by a bank and ditch set off with a wooden palisade. Within were several huts – depending on the size of the family – while the land outside the fence was cultivated, with the

livestock left to run free. Some 40,000 of these forts still exist in Ireland, where they are thought of as the dwelling places of the Faery people and are thus never ploughed or built over.

Chieftains and kings lived in larger versions of these forts, called *raths*. They were heavily defended and patrolled by warriors in constant readiness for attack. A system of roads connected these greater establishments and a law was enforced which said that they must be tended and kept open on three occasions; in winter, when the land became harsh and cruel; during time of war, when the movement of men was all important; and during the time of the horse-races – for then, as now, the Irish loved to hold races and to bet huge sums on their favourites.

There were something like 150 small kingdoms in Ireland at the time of Fionn and the Fianna. Each had its own ruler and, when allied, these formed a province under a greater king, who in turn owed allegiance to the High King – though this office was not really established until the beginning of the eighth century, some 500 years after the time of the Fianna.

Fionn's lord, Cormac mac Art (who was also, later, his father-in-law) was one of the first and greatest to claim the title. He established his capital at Tara and raised the Fianna from every province in the land, giving each lord a part in the defence of the realm while at the same time strengthening his own position.

The choice of Tara for the High King's seat was no accident. Ancient Ireland was divided into five provinces: Connaught (West), Ulster (North),

Staigue Fort, Co. Kerry, shown in a nineteenth century photograph. A circular rath of the kind once occupied by Irish chieftains during the period when the Fianna were active.

11

The gatehouse of Dun Aongusa, Co. Galway, a fort probably named after Aengus mac Og. Its massive stones bear witness to the wealth of its builders and the style in which they lived.

Leinster (East), Munster (South), Meath (Centre). Tara, traditionally the place of power where all true kings of Ireland were made, was in Meath. Geographically this is nowhere near the centre of the country, but mythologically it was correct.

By the same ancient system of division, the provinces were held responsible for the provision of certain skills among their inhabitants. Thus, Connaught was famed for its learning, Ulster for its warriors, Leinster for prosperity, Munster for music and Meath for kingship. Lists of the people and qualities expected to come out of these places – as though they grew there like cultivated crops – are still extant.

Tara itself, with its great hall, could offer hospitality to a hundred men in the style to which the Celts were accustomed: beer had to flow and meat had to be plentiful. Precise rules governed the seating arrangements of the guests, as they also governed the portions of meat they could be expected to receive. Thus, hunters received a pig's shoulder, as did harpists; while the King's fool, or his doorkeepers, got only chines. The seating plans from ancient manuscripts show both how complex were the rules, and how precise.

The seating arrangement (opposite) in Cormac's banqueting hall at Tara, where Fionn and the Fianna may often have dined. The plan was almost symmetrical, with charioteers, for example, seated in each of the top left-hand and right-hand places. Furthermore, as well as each occupation and profession having its place, each group had specified food for the feast.

Despite his position as overlord of Tara, there were many who refused to accept Cormac's right to call himself High King. He had to establish his right through conquest initially, and even with the support of the Fianna, his tenure was never a strong one. Nonetheless, like all the High Kings then and after, he accepted the complex system of laws governing his occupations and duties. As an ancient manuscript puts it:

12

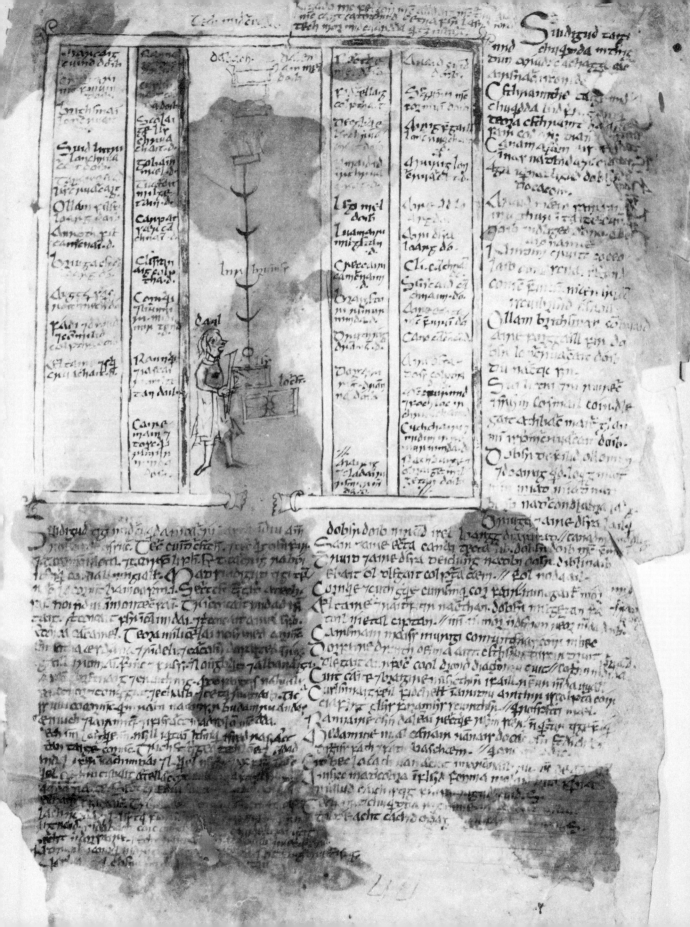

There are seven occupations for a king; Sunday for drinking ale, for he is not a lawful chief who does not distribute ale every Sunday; Monday for judgement, for the adjustment of the people; Tuesday at chess; Wednesday seeing greyhounds coursing; Thursday at marriage duties; Friday at horse-racing; Saturday at giving judgements.

(*The Brehon Laws*)

The fact that two out of the seven are given over to law-making and only one to lovemaking indicates the importance of the former to the Celtic people – indeed they were among the first Western cultures to develop an intricate system of laws governing daily life.

Warriors and Weapons

The Celtic warriors were amongst the fiercest and most terrifying of the ancient world. Their culture gave the warrior pride of place and expected him to perform bravely at all times. He often went into battle naked, both from bravado and as a magical act in which he expected to be protected by his gods. With his hair whitened with lime, combed into fantastic shapes, his body patterned with tattoos, he always attacked furiously, screaming his war shout or chanting extravagant boasts of his own past deeds of bravery.

The Celts were also headhunters, believing the head to be the seat of the soul, possession of which lent strength to oneself. Accounts of warriors with belts of skulls, severed heads decorating their chariots and horse harnesses abound. In earlier times, there had been a widespread use of the chariot in which the warriors would career up and down in front of their enemies, flinging spears or shouting insults until they were met by a champion from the opposing side. The Fianna, however, never seem to have used chariots. They were light-clad, mobile and ranged freely across the country on their swift horses, dismounting to give battle with swords and spears.

These weapons were of iron, long and heavy-bladed swords with bronze hilts made in three parts – guard, grip and pommel. They were an improvement over the earlier bronze-bladed weapons which tended to be more flexible. We hear of warriors straightening these beneath their feet during battle. The average sword was 3 feet in length with the hilt being some 6 inches of this. Blades tended to be about 2½ inches broad, tapering to $1\frac{7}{8}$ inches. They were used to cut and hack rather than to stab, and were carried in bronze sheaths with bronze chapes, which enabled their users to hold the scabbard behind one knee and draw the sword forth one-handed, whilst holding their shield with the other. Later, shorter swords became the fashion, worn slung across the upper part of the body. The Fianna would probably have used both kinds.

14

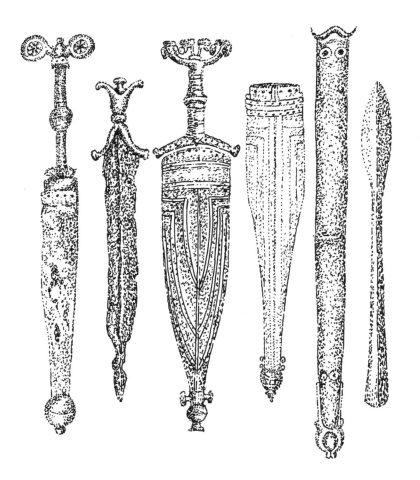

Knives, some with bone-hilts, others with bronze, were also carried, though not everyone would have used both knives and swords. Spears were long, slender-shafted with heavy warheads, some consisting of a central spike with several sharp phalanges opening out from the central blade. These went into the body easily but always tore on being drawn out. Slings would also have been used, though less frequently than sword and spear; and there are stories of balls made from the brains of enemies being used as sling-shots.

There was little armour of any kind, mail shirts being exceedingly rare and expensive. Leather shirts and breeches, some oversown with plates of metal or waxed linen, would have been worn by the wealthier warriors. However, to wear armour of any kind would have militated against the Celtic warrior's sense of honour.

Fionn is described as preparing for the Battle of Gabhra as follows:

Then rose the royal chief of the *fiana* of Ireland and Scotland and of the Saxons and Britons, of Lewis and Norway and of the hither islands, and put on his battle-dress of combat and contest, even a thin, silken shirt of wonderful, choice satin of the fair-cultivated Land of

(Opposite and above) *a selection of Celtic weapons coming from many different sites and periods. This array indicates the variety and artistic qualities instilled by the Celts into their tools of war.*

15

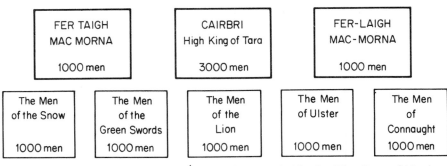

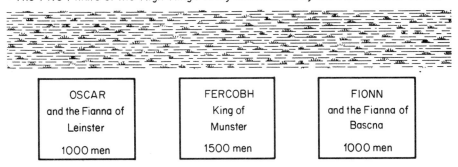

FER TAIGH MAC MORNA 1000 men	CAIRBRI High King of Tara 3000 men	FER-LAIGH MAC-MORNA 1000 men

The Men of the Snow 1000 men	The Men of the Green Swords 1000 men	The Men of the Lion 1000 men	The Men of Ulster 1000 men	The Men of Connaught 1000 men

The Five Pillars of the High King's Army Commanded by the Five Sons of Ureriu

OSCAR and the Fianna of Leinster 1000 men	FERCOBH King of Munster 1500 men	FIONN and the Fianna of Bascna 1000 men

Plan of the Battle of Gabhra, which took place in 297 A.D. on high moorland near the Hill of Gabhra in Co. Meath. This depiction is based on surviving manuscript sources and on records of the names of those who fought. Whether the battle actually took place at this site and in this manner can neither be proved nor disproved.

Promise over the face of his white skin; and outside over that he put his twenty-four waxed, stout shirts of cotton, firm as a board, about him, and on the top of those he put his beautiful, plaited, three-meshed coat of mail of cold refined iron, and around his neck his graven gold-bordered breastplate, and about his waist he put a stout corslet with a decorated, firm belt with gruesome images of dragons, so that it reached from the thick of his thighs to his arm-pit, whence spears and blades would rebound. And his stout-shafted martial five-edged spears were placed over against the king, and he put his gold-hafted sword in readiness on his left, and he grasped his broad-blue, well-ground Norse lance, and upon the arched expanse of his back he placed his emerald-tinted shield with flowery designs and with variegated, beautiful bosses of pale gold, and with delightful studs of bronze, and with twisted stout chains of old silver; and to protect the hero's head in battle he seized his crested, plated, four-edged helmet of beautiful, refined gold with bright, magnificent, crystal gems and with flashing, full-beautiful, precious stones which had been set in it by the hands of master-smiths and great artists.

(*Fianaigecht* trans: Kuno Meyer)

Helmets varied in form, but were at base a bronze cap with horns or peaks added. At the Battle of Mucrine (250 A.D.), some were described as 'crested' – perhaps in the likeness of Roman helmets which some well-travelled mercenaries would have seen. Shields, either oblong or round, were made from wicker work or hide. These were strengthened by strips of iron and bronze, and sometimes had a central boss which could be highly decorated.

Other weapons included battle-axes, used for throwing or hand-to-hand combat; and bronze or iron-tipped maces, often with elaborately carved hilts.

Weapons were sharpened on a ceremonial whetstone known as the 'Pillar of Combat' which was also struck in time of war or to announce single combat. It was set up outside the King's hall on the green.

The Fianna were the greatest hunters in Ireland, famed for their horsemanship and courage in the chase. The greatest of all the hunters was Fionn himself, here in the act of spearing his quarry, his favourite hounds by his side.

Bronze helmet crest in the shape of a boar, showing the kind of beast often hunted by the Fianna. One such, the Boar of Ben Bulben, caused the death of Diarmuid O'Duibne, the greatest of Fionn's heroes.

War bands such as the Fianna all comprised three classes of men, who were bound by law to give a certain number of days' weapon-service to their king or overlord. These formed the main part of the war band, but were supplemented by the mercenaries which the king maintained at a fixed rate of pay. These were drawn from many places, including Britain and Scandinavia, and were much hated by the irregular soldiery, who, in most cases, did their stint of service and hurried home to wife and harvest. Men of uncertain allegiance would sometimes be paired with a 'safe' man in battle, often being yoked to him by the leg!

The King had an *aire-echta*, or champion, who avenged family insults or murders, and who was responsible, in time of war, for guarding the most vulnerable passes into the King's domain. He had five men to serve under him, while the King himself had a personal guard (*lucht-tighe*) of personal warriors.

Female warriors were not unknown among the Celts, though they seem to have primarily served in the capacity of trainers. Many of the greatest heroes were taught by women: Cuchulainn by Scathach, who ran a kind of warrior-school; Fionn by Liath, whose training methods included throwing him into deep water, to teach him how to swim, and racing with him until whoever was the faster would strike the loser with a peeled wand. Women also seem to have cared for the sick and those too old or severely wounded to fight. Hostels for the sick were administered at public expense.

As part of their task was the defence of Ireland's coast, the Fianna had an intricate system of look-outs and signals posted at clifftop, ford and passes of strategic importance. Signals were passed by relays of runners (often women) or by beacon-fires at night. The Fianna could thus be at the site of an attack in record time. Battles were often very organised affairs, joined by mutual agreement on certain days and at specified times.

Although this decorated Iron Age scabbard dates from a period several hundred years before Fionn, the stylized images of mounted warriors give a good idea of how the Fianna may well have looked.

Diarmuid, Fotla and Conan Maol held the Ford of the Quicken Trees against hundreds of Fionn's enemies, whilst he and the rest of the Fianna were kept in enchanted imprisonment in the Hostel of the Quicken Trees.

Camps must have resembled impromptu fairgrounds, such as the Irish erected at certain festival times, everything ordered in streets of booths or tents with the King's tent set on an eminence and trenches with palisades thrown up round the whole.

Before battle, each warrior took a stone and these were piled in cairns. Afterwards, those stones not claimed enabled the number of the dead to be calculated.

Thus, the Fianna kept Ireland safe and law-abiding throughout their existence. Despite our lack of detailed historical knowledge, we can say without doubt that they must have been one of the finest bands of fighting men ever to have existed.

This short sword is a product of the Celtic Hallstatt culture. It would have been carried by a nobleman of the kind who served with the Fianna.

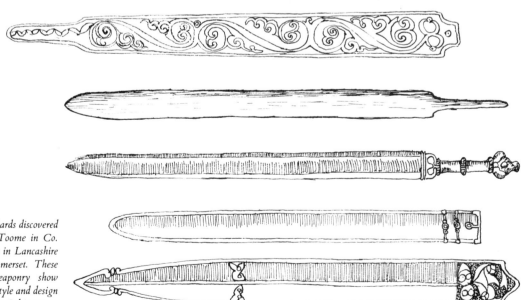

Swords and scabbards discovered as far apart as Toome in Co. Antrim, Worton in Lancashire and Mere in Somerset. These examples of weaponry show how defined the style and design became during the Celtic era.

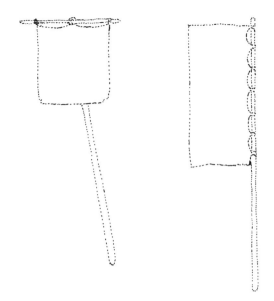

The Heroes of the Fianna

Nothing quite like the Fianna has existed before or since. Unlike other war bands of the time they were drawn from every province and part of Ireland. The owed allegiance only to Fionn (though they must in fact have existed before, since Fionn's father Cumhail was their commander before him) and through him to the High King. But they did not spend all the year fighting; from Beltain to Samhain (April to October) they hunted and lived off the land, seldom remaining in one place more than a few nights. The rest of the year, they were liable to be billeted on noble or freeborn people without charge – part of their wages for the protection of the land. What their regular wages were is not recorded, though Fionn once speaks of giving one man 'three times fifty ounces of gold and silver in one day'.

Certainly they were well clothed:

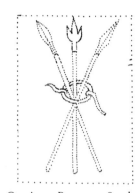

Oscar's Banner Squab Ghabhaidh Terrible Sheaf.

And there were fifty of the best sewing-women in Ireland brought together in a rath on Magh Feman, under the charge of a daughter of the king of Britain, and they used to be making clothing for the Fianna through the whole of the year. And three of them, that were king's daughters, used to be making music for the rest on a little silver harp; and there was a very great candle-stick of stone in the middle of the rath, for they were not willing to kindle a fire more than three times a year for fear the smoke and the ashes might harm the needlework.

(*Gods and Fighting Men*: Gregory)

Goll Mac Morna's Banner Fulang Doghra Prop of Lamentation.

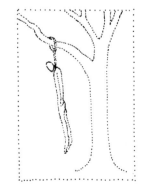

Though they were thus well cared for, the Fianna lived a wandering life, rarely staying in one place more than a few days. For this reason, there are many places in Ireland and Scotland which are associated with the Fianna – yet few large fortresses or sites carry their name. Fionn himself had his headquarters at the Hill of Almu (or Allan) in Kildare, though there are no signs today of the fortified Dunn from which the Fianna once rode to hunt and battle. From there, riding in small bands, the whole of Ireland and much

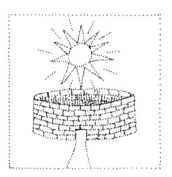

Oisin's Banner Dun Naomhtha
Sacred Citadel.

Fionn's Banner Dealbh Ghreine
Image of the Sun.

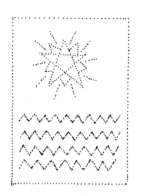

Diarmuid O'Duibne's Banner
Loch Luinneach   *The Lively*
Light.

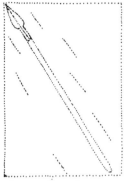

The Raighne Clan's Banner
Aoincheannach   Oir   *The*
Single-headed Golden One.

of Scotland was their province – though they remained always ready to answer the *Diord Fionn*, the Call of Fionn.

Many of the Fianna were of otherworldy origin – strange folk who came to take service with Fionn mac Cumhail for a year, and who at the end of that time vanished again into the mists of Tir-nan-Og. People like Dubh, Agh, and Ilar (Black, Battle and Eagle) who undertook as Gregory says to 'do the watching for all the Fianna of Ireland and of Alban' or to 'take the weight of every fight and every battle that will come their way'. While the third offered to 'meet every troublesome thing that might come to my master . . . And I have a pipe with me . . . and all the men of the world would sleep at the sound of it, and they in their sickness.'

Among the most famous of the Fianna were Caoilte mac Ronan, Fionn's nephew, who was famed for his swiftness of foot – at full speed he appeared like three men and could overtake the March wind. There was also Diarmuid ui Duibhne who 'never knew weariness of foot, nor shortness of breath, nor, whether in going out or coming in, ever flagged.' He also possessed a beauty spot which made him irresistible to women. Another, Conan Maol, began as an enemy of the Fianna and had to pay a fine for his part in the death of Fionn's father. Later he joined the Fianna but continued to mock them with his 'foul-mouthed tongue'. Goll mac Morna was also Fionn's enemy at the start, but he relinquished the leadership of the Fianna in Fionn's favour and became his faithful follower. His huge and cheerful humour was famed among all the company of the Fianna.

These and many more made up the great company, whose motto was:

> Truth in our hearts.
> Strength in our hands.
> Consistency in our tongues.

Requirements for admission to the Fianna were rigorous and demanding. Among other tests the would-be applicant had to be able to leap over a pole held at head high and knee high without breaking stride, pull a thorn from his heel while running across rough country, and to dodge spears hurled at him by a ring of warriors while he was half buried in the earth. Small wonder

Mac Ronan's Banner Lamh Dhearg
Red Hand.

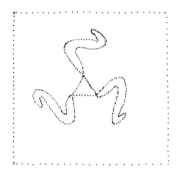

Caoilte's Banner Tri Chosa
Three Legs.

Faolan's Banner Coinneal
Chatha *Torch of Battle.*

that the Fianna were the finest body of fighting men in Ireland and Scotland, who were never defeated until their enemies banded together to overthrow them at the battle of Gabhra in the year 284.

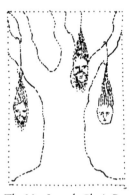

The Mac Lugach Clan's Banner Graobh Fhuileach *The Bloody Tree.*

The Heritage of Story

The stories of Fionn and his heroes are as old as the hills of Ireland, though they were not in fact written down until the early Middle Ages. Before that they circulated orally. When the Irish Gaels (called *Scotti*) infiltrated into the West of Scotland (then the dwelling-place of the Picts) in the first century A.D. they took with them the tales of Fionn mac Cumhail. So, in time these stories came to be as much a part of Scottish Highland folklore as that of Ireland.

By the tenth century, when the great hero-cycle of Cuchulainn and the Red Branch Knights was first being recorded, tales of Fionn were being told by the common people by the fireside all over Ireland. These stories were to them what the tales and songs of Robin Hood were to the Saxon peasants in England a hundred years later. They have continued to be told and retold right into the present – with new stories still being added in Scotland and Ireland as late as the nineteenth century.

Literary references began to appear around the eleventh century, and in the twelfth this blossomed into a fully fledged series of ballads about Fionn and his warrior band. This shows parallels between the Robin Hood ballads already mentioned, the Arthurian cycle, and the Homeric ballads upon which the Greek poet based his great works the *Illiad* and the *Odyssey*.

By the sixteenth century, new stories were being written, and Fionn's fame had outstripped that of other, once more famous heroes. But Fionn's greatest moment came in the eighteenth century, when the Scottish poet James Macpherson (1736–1796) wrote a series of epic poems based on the stories of Oisin (Fionn's son) and the hero he called Fingal. Had he chosen simply to publish these under his own name they might have vanished without trace. Instead, however, he elected to pass them off as translations from the ancient Scots and Irish Gaelic. This so excited the antiquary-mad populace of the time that these books became best sellers and placed the name of Fionn and Oisin in the minds of a vast number of readers. Both Napoleon and Goethe loved to read these stirring tales, believing them to be real. Indeed, they caused such a revival of interest in ancient Celtic stories that they inadvertently touched off what was to become known as the Celtic Twilight, a literary movement which attracted writers as varied as Matthew Arnold, W. B. Yeats, Fiona Macleod and Lady Augusta Gregory, to whom we owe our own present day knowledge of the Fionn cycle.

Macpherson's forgeries, for such they were in time recognized to be, touched off such a furore in literary circles that people almost came to blows as they alternately attacked or defended the poet's scholarship. In fact, Macpherson had used some original sources for his work, adapting and altering them to suit the taste of the time – just as all the many story-tellers had done since the time of the Fianna.

Today, the Fionn cycle is possibly the least well known of the great mythical cycles. Yet its range is as wide as any of the tales of Arthur, Cuchulainn, Charlemagne or Sigurd. There are stories of heroism to be sure, but there are stories which contain elements of high comedy, high tragedy, magic and love. The story of Diarmuid and Grainne and their flight across Ireland from the wrath of Fionn is one of the great love stories of all time, and certainly influenced the composition of its more famous sibling story of Tristan and Isolt in the Arthurian saga. The magic, rich and otherworldly, is of a high quality – we may think of the intervention of Angus Og in the Diarmuid saga, or the coming of Niamh of the Golden Hair – or indeed of Oisin's sojourn in the Land of Youth and his strange meeting with the monk Patrick. There are tales of honour and treachery, truth and falsehood, strength and weakness; subtle stories and stories written out of the passionate soul of the Gaels.

The early stories of the Fianna written in christian times show an easy-going fellowship and understanding between pagan and christian, with Oisin and St Patrick swapping stories and the latter having the deeds of Fionn recorded in his monastery. Later, this decayed into ill-feeling and almost buffoonish characteristics in which Oisin can say that if he saw his son Oscar fighting with God and saw Oscar fall then he would have to admit that God was the stronger of the two! In this way the stories of Fionn parallel the changes which took place in Ireland over the centuries. Yet they remained a guide to the earliest times and enshrined within them the memory of the people, without which no land is called living. In a text called *Acallam na Senorach* (the Colloquy of the Ancients) composed around 1200 A.D., many of the stories of Fionn are combined into a rich tapestry. Oisin and Caoilte, supposedly still living in the fifth century, travel about Ireland with the Saint,

These two Gaulish images of Celtic hair styles give an excellent idea of the care and attention lavished by the Celtic warrior class on their appearance. Beards were neatly trimmed and hair dressed to the best effect.

22

and at every place they visit recall another story of the Fianna. In this way, the stories and associations with places are enshrined in a form that ensures they will be remembered for at least as long as the stories are read and retold.

In another text, this is taken a step further. Caoilte, who was famed for his swiftness of foot, has to rescue Fionn from the clutches of a king, and he is given the seemingly impossible task of finding two of every animal and bird in Ireland and bringing them to the king's court. He does so – not without some difficulty even for a hero of Caoilte's stature, and in the text we find a list of the creatures and the places where he found them. The ancient names become like a song, chanted by a bard before the kings of ancient Ireland, and the land itself rises before our eyes as we listen to the great catalogue of names:

It is with the flocks of birds he began, though they were scattered in every part, and from them he went on to the beasts. And he gathered together two of every sort, two ravens from Fiodh da Bheann; two wild ducks from Loch na Seillein; two foxes from Slieve Cuilinn; two wild oxen from Burren; two swans from blue Dobhran; two owls from the wood of Faradhruim; two polecats from the branchy wood on the side of Druim da Raoin, the Ridge of the Victories; two gulls from the strand of Loch Leith; four woodpeckers from white Brosna; two plovers from Carraigh Dhain; two thrushes from Leith Lomard; two wrens from Dun Aoibh; two herons from Corrain Cleibh; two eagles from Carraig of the stones; two hawks from Fiodh Chonnach; two sows from Loch Meilghe; two water-hens from Loch Erne; two moorhens from Monadh Maith; two sparrow-hawks from Dubhloch; two stonechats from Magh Cuillean; two tomtits from Magh Tuaillainn, two swallows from Sean Abhla; two cormorants from Aith Cliath; two wolves from Broit Cliathach; two blackbirds from the Strand of the Two Women; two roebucks from Luachair Ire; two pigeons from Ceas Chuir; two nightingales from Leiter Ruadh; two starlings from green-sided Teamhair; two rabbits from Sith Dubh Donn; two wild pigs from Cluaidh Chuir; two cuckoos from Drom Daibh; two lapwings from Leanain na Furraich; two woodcocks from Craobh Ruadh; two hawks from the Bright Mountain; two grey mice from Luimneach; two otters from the Boinn; two larks from the Great Bog; two bats from the Cave of the Nuts; two badgers from the province of Ulster; two landrail from the banks of the Sionnan; two wagtails from Port Lairrge; two curlews from the harbour of Gallimh; two hares from Muirthemne; two deer from Sith Buidhe; two peacocks from Magh Mell; two cormorants from Ath Cliath; two eels from Duth Dur; two goldfinches from Slieve na-n Eun; two birds of slaughter from Magh Bhuilg; two bright swallows from Granard; two redbreasts from the Great Wood; two rock-cod from Cala Chairge; two sea-pigs from the great sea; two wrens from Mios an Chuil; two salmon from Eas Mhic Muirne; two clean deer from Gleann na Smoil; two cows from Magh Mor; two cats from the Cave of Cruachan; two sheep from bright Sidhe Diobhlain; two pigs of the pigs of the son of Lir; a ram and a crimson sheep from Innis.

Such is the power of the Fionn saga to move and transport us to other times

A bronze cult chariot from Spain depicting a mounted huntsman with hound in pursuit of a boar. The Fianna were great hunters and spent much of their time in the chase.

and other places, where the old magic of the Celts still lives on and where we find ourselves entering another kind of world – one where the old values and strengths of the heroes may be ours for a while, and perhaps enable us to view our own world with new eyes.

Fionn's Magic

It used to be said that Fionn had wisdom and knowledge far beyond that of ordinary mortals, and there are three tales which tell how he came by it. In the first of these a man of the *sidhe*, the Faery People, stole food from the Fianna, for which insult and nuisance Fionn gave chase. But while he was in pursuit of the man, he saw a woman of the *sidhe*, who had come out of the mound to fetch water. When she saw Fionn she too fled, so that he gave chase to her also. But she was too quick for Fionn and reached the safety of the mound. But Fionn was so close behind her that as the gates of the Faery Hill closed shut, he caught his thumb in the crack of the door. So great was the pain and so sudden, that Fionn pulled his thumb back and put it into his mouth. But because his thumb had been in the Otherworld, even if only for a moment, from this came all his knowledge.

On another occasion Fionn was hunting near the Well of the Moon, that was watched over by three women of Faery, the daughters of Beag son of Buan. The well supposedly had the power to grant knowledge which was not for ordinary men. Thus as Fionn came closer and closer, the three women ran out to distract him and prevent him coming near the well. One of the women happened to be carrying a jar of water, and she threw this at Fionn to stop him coming any further. Some of the water went into his mouth in that moment, and it is supposed that all knowledge came to him.

The third story is told later elsewhere in this book but again the outcome is the same: Fionn acquires wisdom by supernatural means, and has thereafter only to put his thumb or two fingers into his mouth to receive instant illumination.

The story is an ancient one – a similar account is given of the Welsh poet Taliesin, who happened to receive three drops of the Brew of Inspiration from the cauldron of the Sow-Goddess Ceridwen. Taliesin became the greatest poet of the age and was famed for his wisdom. Fionn's knowledge however is more gnomic, more homely, as in this example, where he gives advice to a would-be champion of the Fianna:

If you have a mind to be a good champion, be quiet in a great man's house; . . . do not beat your hound without a cause; do not bring a charge against your wife without having knowledge of her guilt; do not hurt a fool in fighting, for he is without his wits. Do not find fault with high-up persons; do not stand up to take part in a quarrel; have no dealings with a bad man or a foolish man. Let two-thirds of your gentleness be showed to women and to little children that are creeping on the floor, and to men of learning that make the poems, and do not be rough with the common people . . . Do not threaten or speak big words, for it is a shameful thing to speak stiffly unless you carry it out afterwards . . . Do not be a bearer of lying stories, or a tale-bearer of lying stories, or a tale-bearer that is always chattering . . .

(trans: Lady Gregory)

Perhaps nowhere in ancient literature has more sound advice than this been given. It is unique to Fionn and is part of the enduring fascination of the cycle.

Among the Celts there were said to be three kinds of wisdom or poetic utterance, and with their love of codifying things they classed them under specific headings. There was *Teinm Laida* (illumination of song); *Imbas Farosna* (knowledge which illumines); and *Dichetual Dichennaib* (extemporary incantation or incantation from the ends of the fingers). Much speculation has been lavished on the exact meaning of these terms. *Teinm Laida* seems to relate to inspired utterance, possibly in trance, of the kind practised by poets. *Imbas Farosna* may be devination by way of the poet's wand, whereas *Dichetual Dichennaib* seems to refer to the insertion of two or more fingers in the mouth, clearly the same action as that performed by Fionn when he wishes to know something. Another method was the placing of the hands in a certain fashion on the poet's staff, which performs much the same function as that of the wizard or magician – poetry and magic being still indistinguishable at this time.

One explanation may lead us to ogham, an ancient form of writing consisting of groups of marks placed at intervals along a straight edge. They are found carved on stones all over Ireland and Scotland. There were many kinds of ogham, which was also associated with magic and poetry. Finger ogham was a kind of sign language which enabled poets to talk to each other without being detected. Ogham carved on wooden sticks seems reminiscent of *Imbas Farosna* and may be the origin of this mysterious method of acquiring knowledge.

Newgrange is one of the finest ancient sites in Ireland. Although it dates from a period many hundreds of years before Fionn, it was still in use as a sacred site. This was how the Fianna envisaged the dwelling places of the Tuatha de Danaan – the Sidhs *or Hollow Hills of legend. Newgrange of Brugh na Boyne was the home of Aengus mac Og, the Otherworldly patron of Diarmuid.*

Fionn seems always to have used his own skills wisely and well, and his wisdom becomes a bright thread running through the tapestry of the deeds of the Fianna.

*   *   *

It is time now to tell some of those stories, for in no other way can we come to know and understand the magic they wield, which has kept their memory green in the lives of story-tellers from their own time to this. In retelling these stories of the Fianna there is a deliberate attempt, as far as possible, to preserve the feel and spirit of the originals, occasionally quoting from earlier translations. However, in keeping with all storytelling, individual touches are added, and much has had to be omitted, since to tell all the stories would require a book several times the length of this one.

Oisin and St Patrick

One day the monk Patrick came to the Hostel of the Red Ridge to say Mass, and while he was chanting the orisons some people came to him and said: 'There is a wonder that you should see.' They took Patrick to a little smoky bothy nearby and showed him the man that lay sleeping within. A great warrior he seemed, larger in limb than any man there, for all that his hair and beard were white and his body heavy with age. At his side lay a great sword with a broad iron blade and a hilt of bronze, and leaning against the wall of the bothy was a long straight-shafted spear with a heavy head and a shield of the finest hide with bosses of iron. By the side of that lay his great war-cap of leather strengthened with bronze.

'Whence came this man?' asked Patrick, and the people told him that he had come riding out of the mists one morning on a great tall horse and had offered to move a great stone that lay in the middle of a field, that not ten of their own number could move. And in so doing he broke the girth of his horse and fell to the earth, at which the people witnessed a great change, for until that moment he had seemed to them a hero in the finest flower of his days, but when he arose from the earth he was as he now seemed, a hoary old man, still stronger than most of them, but deep in years. Since that moment he had not spoken a word, but had lain in the hut with his face turned to the wall.

It seemed to Patrick that he had heard tell of warriors such as this, and that they had lived in pagan times, so he decided to question the man, and entering the hut he awoke him.

'I am Patrick, and I serve the Christ. By what name are you known?'

'I am Oisin, son of Fionn, whom I serve. I am one of the Fianna of Ireland.'

Patrick looked at the old warrior in amazement. 'I have heard of the Fianna' he said, 'but it is more than three centuries since they were in Ireland.'

'Then it is true,' said the warrior. 'They are all dead and I am the last of the Fianna' and he wept for a long while.

At length he raised his head and asked: 'I would know of this time in which I find myself, for it seems unlike the days when I was young.'

'I shall be happy to tell you,' answered Patrick. 'But first I would have you tell me how you have lived these past three hundred years, when all of your kin lie dead?'

'That is soon told,' said Oisin sadly, and he spoke at length of the days of the Fianna and how he had come to love Niamh, a woman of the *sidhe*, the Lordly Ones who live in the land of Tir-nan-Og. And on a time she had come for him, to take him to her own land and people, taking him up on the back of a steed as white as milk.

'And fast as were the horses of the Fianna, the mount of Niamh was faster, and in truth it seemed that the earth fell away beneath its hooves, and that when we reached the sea it did not pause but galloped over the tops of the waves as though they were a hard roadway. Many were the wonders we saw,' said Oisin. 'Cities and courts and palaces of silver and gold that seemed to float above the sea: and deer running hard with a red-eared, white-bodied hound following on. At another time, coming towards us, we saw a woman on a black horse who had a golden apple in her right hand. And following after her a youth on a white horse who wore a crimson cloak and carried a sword of gold. And they passed us on the right hand. But in time we came to the land of youth itself, and of that I must speak either no words at all, or continue talking for all the days that are left to me. So I will but say that it is always green spring and golden summer there, and no sickness is there, nor

The Kells High Cross in Co. Meath shows the crucifixion and the wounding of Christ by the spear of Longinus, the centurion. Christianity overlaid many aspects of pagan Ireland; whatever was loved and respected of the old order was assimilated into the new ways. The stories of Fionn and his Fianna were no exception. Oisin's return from the Otherworld of pagan Ireland into the newly Christian land of Patrick's conversion enabled these stories to be widely transcribed.

death, and the folk who dwell there are perilously fair, and garbed in finest silk and with gold upon them, heavy at neck and wrist.

'There I stayed, and it seemed to me that only a year passed, which I spent with Niamh of the golden hair. Then upon a time I took thought of Fionn my father and of my companions, and the need arose in me to see them again. And Niamh looked upon me sadly and bade her women prepare her steed. "For" she said, "I see that I cannot keep you here. But only remember this, that when you are come again into the land of Ireland, do not dismount or let your foot so much as touch the earth, lest you see me no more nor return to Tir-nan-Og."

'So I mounted upon the milk white steed and returned as I had come, riding the tops of the waves as though they were a road; and I saw again the woman with the golden apple, followed by the youth with the scarlet cloak, but this time they were coming towards the Land of Youth, and passed me upon the left hand.

'So at last I came to the shore of Ireland and it seemed changed. I rode everywhere in search of the Fianna, until I came to this place and chanced to set foot on the earth. Until that moment I had been in the brightness of my youth; but from that moment I have been as you see me now. And the white steed of Tir-nan-Og turned and galloped away from me, back, as I believe, to the place where Niamh of the golden hair awaited him.

'So you have my story, Talkend' said Oisin, calling Patrick by the name which means 'shaven one'.

Patrick sat in silence a long while, thinking of all that he had heard, and then he said: 'Come with me, Oisin son of Fionn, and when you are in my house we shall talk more of these things.'

And so Oisin accompanied Patrick upon the road back to his monastery, and as they walked the two men by turn talked and were silent, and in that time they found the beginning of a friendship between them, and when the two angels that were Patrick's guardians visited him at night, they told him there was no evil in the ancient warrior. So that when they came at last to Ard Macha, Patrick gave over a wattled cell to Oisin, and spent many days and some nights in talk with him.

He found the warrior willing enough to listen to stories of the Christ and his Disciples, though there was no inclining in him towards following the new faith. And if at times they spoke harshly together because of this, at others they talked as friends.

In time Patrick ordered one of his scribes to leave off his work transcribing the Gospels into the Irish tongue and instead to write down the stories of the Fianna: 'For there is a great wisdom in this Fionn, even though he was a pagan, and such things should not be forgotten in Ireland, less it should become a lesser place.'

And of the stories that Oisin told, that the monk of Ard Macha wrote down, these are some that are told again in this time and this place, lest we also become smaller people, and forget what once was.

The Boyhood Deeds of Fionn

Fionn's father, Cumhail, was the first captain of the Fianna, but he was slain in battle by the sons of Morna. Muirne, Fionn's mother, took her small son, that was but a few months old, to the woods of Sleive Bladhma to be cared for by two women, Bodhmall the Druidess and the Liath Luachra, who was both a warrior and a teacher of warriors.

And Fionn saw his mother only once again, when he was six years old, but otherwise he saw no people at all save his two guardians, and they taught him wisdom and strength, which are the two attributes of all heroes. And when he was come to his youngmanhood they taught him to run and found him fleet of foot and sure in his going. And they taught him to swim, and found him at home there in the water as a fish; and on another time they took him into a field where there were hares and instructed him to let none escape from there. And none did, so that they declared him a worthy champion, though he had as yet fought no battle except in trial against Liath Luachra.

At last his guardians said that he must go away: 'For the Sons of Morna are seeking abroad to kill you.' And Fionn learned all the truth of his parentage and went into Connacht in search of Crimhall, his father's brother, that was believed to live there.

On the way he fell in with some youths who were swimming in a lake, and he outswam them all in contest, for which they were displeased. But one among them saw how fair he seemed in his body and called him *fionn* which means 'fair', and thus he came by that name, for until that time he had none.

Then Fionn went into Carraighe and took service with a king who all unknown to him had married his mother. And one night he played chess with the king and won seven games together. Then the king looked at him narrowly and said: 'You are the son of Cumhail, that was lord of the Fianna. I bid you depart, for I wish not to have it said that you were killed while under my protection.'

So Fionn travelled on, still searching for Crimhall, and it chanced that he met a woman who wept tears of blood for the death of her son at the hands of a great warrior who dwelled nearby. So Fionn went up against this champion and slew him, thus fighting his first fight, and the man he slew had been the first to strike a blow at his father Cumhail, and had carried off his treasure bag.

Now this bag was made of crane skin and contained many magical items and much wisdom besides. When he had it Fionn knew by its aid how to find Crimhall, who was living with the last of the old Fianna who had refused to serve under the Sons of Morna. They knew him at once when they saw him, for he had the look of Cumhail about him, and bore the crane-bag. Very glad they were to see him and swore that they would follow him only.

But Fionn had a thirst now for the knowledge he had tasted through the magic of the crane-bag, so he went to take service with a poet and seer named Finegas, who lived by the side of the Boinne river. But Fionn did not use his own name; he took that of Deimne, and for seven years he remained with Finegas, learning all that he had to teach.

Now Finegas had stayed there by the side of the Boinne, watching for the day when he would catch the Salmon of Wisdom, for there was a prophecy that said he would eat of it. And at last, when Fionn had been with him just five years, he caught it and gave it to his young apprentice to cook. 'But see that you eat none of the flesh,' he said.

After a time, Fionn came with the cooked fish and the old poet looked at him and said: 'Have you eaten any of the fish?'

Fionn shook his head. 'No – but as I was cooking it I burned my thumb and put it into my mouth to ease the pain.'

Then Finegas gave him the whole fish and said, 'Your name is not Deimne, it is Fionn, and it was of you that the prophecy spoke.'

So Fionn ate all of the fish and had of it all the knowledge of the nine hazels of wisdom from beside the Well of Wonder that is beneath the sea. And thereafter he had only to put his thumb into his mouth to know whatever thing he wished, because of which he became known throughout Ireland – not only for his strength, but also for his wisdom.

Now that he was come into the fulness of his manhood, Fionn went straight to the High King, Cormac mac Art, at his hall in Tara and announced that he was the son of Cumhail, come to claim his place in the Fianna and to serve Cormac. And though the Sons of Morna murmured amongst themselves – especially Goll, the eldest, who was now the captain of the Fianna, Cormac smiled upon the young hero and took him into his service.

*   *   *

Now this was near the time of Samhain, and every year for the past nine years at this time had come a warrior of the Tuatha de Danaan, from *Sidhe Finnachaidh*, and he had burned the roof of Tara with his magic. None might withstand him because of the Faery music he played that caused all the warriors to fall into a deep sleep.

When he heard of this, Fionn came before the King and said that he would rid Tara of this trouble forever, providing that in return his inheritance be recognised. And this the King swore to do upon the surety of all the tributary kings of Ireland and of his royal Druids.

That night, before the warrior of the *sidhe* was destined to appear, one of the High King's men, Fiacha son of Conga, who had served with Cumhail and had a fondness for his son, came to Fionn and offered him help: 'For it is Aillen, son of Midhna that comes this night, and none may resist him without help. But I have a spear which can kill him, in the hands of the right man.'

So Fiacha brought the spear to Fionn, and the property of it was this: that when the cover was taken off the blade, it made a sound of warfare, and if it was laid against the forehead of the warrior who bore it, he would be afflicted

30

by no evil magic. So Fionn took the spear and went out against Aillen mac Midhna, and slew him. He struck off his head and took it back to Tara and fastened it upon a pole for all to see.

When day came, and the High King and his men woke from the sleep of enchantment which Aillen had caused to fall upon them, Cormac called Fionn before him and solemnly invested him with the captaincy of the Fianna. And to Goll mac Morna, who had held that post since the death of Cumhail, he made this offer: 'Will you stay and serve under Fionn mac Cumhail, or will you suffer banishment from Ireland for ever?'

And Goll, who had but one eye, looked with his good one at the young warrior and bowed his head. 'I will stay and serve with Fionn, son of Cumhail. And if I betray him, let me be straightway killed for it.'

Nor did Goll ever betray his captain, but became one of his foremost warriors in time to come.

Thus Fionn became captain of the Fianna, and never in its history or in the history of Ireland has there been such a company of warriors.

How Fionn Got His Grey Hair

Now all the Fianna were great hunters, and none more than Fionn himself, who had two great hounds, Bran and Sgeolan, who came to him from the enchanted realms. And one day they were hunting near Allmu of the White Walls where Fionn had his chief place in Ireland, and they set up a hind that ran so swiftly before them so that no dog, not even Bran and Sgeolan, could catch her. And it seemed to Fionn, who outpaced all the rest of the Fianna, that the hind was making for Allmu as though in search of sanctuary. Sure enough, when they were close to the walls of the dun, Bran and Sgeolan, who had kept close upon the heels of the hind all the while, gave tongue that they had cornered their quarry. But when Fionn came upon them he saw a strange sight, for instead of falling upon the hind and rending her in twain, the two great hounds were licking it and fawning upon it as though it were a long lost sister. Then Fionn knew that there was magic afoot and commanded the rest of the Fianna to call off their dogs. And he took the hind into Allmu, with her trotting before him, and Bran and Sgeolan bounding at either hand.

That night the hind sat always near Fionn's feet and when he went to his sleeping place, she came and lay by him. And in the night he awoke and saw lying by his side the most beautiful woman he had ever seen and she had the eyes of the hind that had followed him at the end of the chase.

The story she told was this: that she was of the Faery people, the Lordly Ones of Tir-nan-Og, and that one of her kind had desired her, though she had always refused him. So at last he had struck her with his hazel wand and turned her into a hind.

'But now I am with Fionn mac Cumhail I know that I am safe, and I would ask that you allow me to stay,' she said. Fionn looked at the woman and asked her name.

'You may call me Sabha,' said she.

Fionn said, 'Sabha, you may stay here for as long as you will, save only that you agree to be my wife.'

And Sabha looked at Fionn in her turn and said that she would.

So Fionn and Sabha drank the bride-cup together and they were happy for a year, in which time Fionn almost gave up hunting or going afoot from Allmu. But at the end of that time, enemies of Ireland were sighted off the coastline and the Fianna had to ride forth, for it was their task to keep the shores and hills free of wrong-doers or of invasion. And though Sabha begged Fionn not to go, yet go he must, but he bade her remain within Allmu until he returned and to speak with no one not of the court.

So the Fianna rode forth and gave battle to their enemies. They were victorious and came home eagerly – none more so than Fionn, who as Allmu of the White Walls came in view, was already searching the ramparts for a sight of Sabha.

When he could not see her, Fionn's heart gave a great lurch and turned over in his breast, and he rode swiftly into the court demanding to know what had occurred. His steward came forward and told him that not two days after he had ridden out of Allmu, there had come a man that seemed in every way like him, and who had two hounds the like of Bran and Sgeolan with him. And Sabha, on seeing this, gave a cry of joy and fled on swift feet to meet the man. But when she came up to him he suddenly struck her with a hazel wand and she became a hind again and, in that moment, the two hounds vanished away and the man that had the appearance of Fionn changed into a strange dark figure who led the hind away.

Then Fionn was broken hearted, for he knew it was the Faery lord who loved Sabha who had taken her away and he believed that he would never see her again. But for all that he began to search, and many long days he spent combing the hills where he had first had a sight of her. Until at last he began to realize that his quest was in vain, and so turned again to the leadership of the Fianna, which he had allowed to lapse while he searched.

Thus seven years passed and once again Fionn rode to the hunting, and this time the quarry that Bran and Sgeolan discovered was even stranger – a little naked boy wandering in the bracken on the hill of Benbulben. And though Fionn spoke to him, he knew no words of human speech, so Fionn took him back to Allmu and had him cared for and taught to speak, until the day came when he could tell his story.

And this was the way of it: for as long as he could remember he had lived in a cave in the hills with a hind for company. Then one day a dark man had come who seemed to want the hind to go with him, and when she would not, the man struck her with a hazel wand and after that she went, though always looking back to where the little boy stood watching. And though he

The Hill of Almu was Fionn's fortress home. Its white walls were to be seen shining from afar as the Fianna returned from their campaigns, to be welcomed by their companions and families.

wished to go also he might not move so much as a foot until he heard the cry of Fionn's hounds and was discovered by Bran and Sgeolan.

Then Fionn knew that the boy was his own son and the child of Sabha, and that now he would never see her again. Yet he still could not give up entirely and leaving the boy with the Fianna, he went alone to the mound on Slieve Gallion, near Armagh, where he knew the Smith of the *sidhe* dwelt beneath the hill.

Now, unknown to him, Cuillen the Smith had two daughters, Aine and Milucra. Aine had seen Fionn and had evinced a great love for him. But Fionn had eyes only for Sabha and failed even to notice Aine, so that when by her magic she knew Fionn was in that part of Ireland, she determined upon a plan to be avenged upon him.

Thus, when Fionn was nearing Slieve Gallion, he came upon a little dark lough in the shelter of the hills and there beside it was sitting a most beautiful woman, weeping full sore.

'Why do you weep, woman of the white arms?' asked Fionn.

'I have lost a red-gold ring that was the gift of my sweetheart,' answered she. 'And I put a *geise* upon you in the name of all the Fianna of Ireland to find it again for me.'

So Fionn stripped off his clothes and dived into the lake, and three times he swam its length and breadth before he found the ring. But when he swam to the bank and stretched forth an arm to give it to her, the woman snatched it from him and with a high, queer laugh, herself leapt into the water and was gone.

When Fionn tried to climb out of the lough, the moment his foot touched the earth, the strength and youth went from him and he lay upon the ground like a feeble old man. Then great terror fell upon him, and he put his thumb into his mouth in fear that the gift of knowledge was also lost to him. But it was not, and at once he knew who was responsible for his state and he knew also that he could nothing to undo matters.

Thus he remained a long while, scarcely able to care for himself until, at last, the Fianna came seeking him, and seeing the ancient man by the lough, demanded whether he had seen a fair strong man come that way of late.

Fionn answered, 'I have indeed and I was that man,' and he told them all the story of what had happened to him.

Then Caoilte mac Ronan, who was one of his chief warriors, spoke up: 'I say that we should call upon the master of this Faery mound and make him aware of our presence.'

There were cries of agreement from the men of the Fianna, and they went straightway to the Sidhe of Cuillen and began to dig and root at the hill. This they did for three nights and three days, and at the end of that time, Cuillen the Smith himself appeared, bearing a golden cup in his hands, and coldly he bade Fionn drink from it. When he did so, immediately he sprang up hale and strong as ever he had been, save that his once golden hair was now grey as ash. But of Cuillen there was no sign, and then Fionn knew at last that there was

Fionn met his death at the Battle of Gabhra. Having slain all his other adversaries, Fionn finally encountered the five sons of Urgriu, on whose spear points he died.

no seeking Sabha further. Therefore he let his hair remain grey and sought no further recompense of Cuillen. . . .

'And that,' said Oisin, 'is how I came to be born, for my father named me Oisin, which means "Little Deer". But my mother he never saw again in this life, and I returned too late from Tir-nan-Og to tell him of her.'

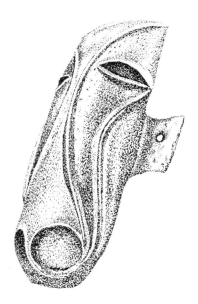

How the Fianna Won Their Horses

This magnificent bronze face-plate horse fitting probably came from a chariot rather than an individual mount; but decorations of this kind could well have been used by the Fianna.

The Fianna were famous horsemen, and used their fine mounts to travel from place to place. Thus they were ever able to be at the site of a battle, or at a pass to be kept against invasion, before any enemy could prepare against them. Yet it was not always so, for in the beginning the Fianna hunted on foot and used to ride small hill ponies, or themselves run all day to arrive where they were needed.

At one time Fionn had with him the son of the King of Britain, that had come to take service with twenty-seven men of his, and they all went hunting together. Fionn sat on the hill of Cnoc Fianna and cheered on his hounds, for he loved nothing so much as to listen to the music of the hunt. The son of the King of Britain, who was named Arthyr, had been set with his men at the head of a valley to watch for the coming of the quarry. When they saw Fionn's two great hounds, Bran and Sgeolan, racing ahead of all the rest, they decided among themselves that they must have these dogs and take them back to Britain. So when the two hounds reached the place where they were, Arthyr and his men called them, put chains upon them and carried them to their ship, sailing swiftly away so that none might know where they had gone.

34

Now when Fionn realised what had occurred he at once set his thumb of knowledge between his teeth and thus he knew who had taken his dogs and where they had gone. Gathering eight men of the Fianna, including Goll mac Morna, Caoilte mac Ronan and his own son, Oisin, he went to the shore and called upon the god Manannan, Lord of the Sea, to send him a ship. For there was a fellowship between Fionn and Manannan that was of old standing. So the boat came, and though there were none on board, yet her sails filled and she crossed the waves like a bird, so that in no time at all the nine men of the Fianna were in Britain. They went to where Arthyr and his men were hunting the lands of Lodan son of Llyr, and there they found the King's son and his men, and with them the two hounds who were most glad to see their master again.

Arthyr feigned friendship to Fionn, suggesting that the theft of the hounds had been but a jest, and inviting the Fianna to dine with him. But soon enough fighting broke out between the two groups and things might have gone ill for the Fianna, who were greatly outnumbered, had not Oisin seized Arthyr round the neck and held him as a shield before him while he slew a dozen of his men. Then Arthyr sued for peace and said that Fionn should have the dogs back and also a gift of two horses – a magnificent grey and a fine chestnut mare that were themselves a gift of his father the King. These Fionn accepted and took them back with him to Ireland; and from their stock came all the mounts of the Fianna thereafter. And it is also said that from them another king of Britain, also named Arthur, took the notion of using horses in battle, which helped him to defeat his enemies just as it had helped Fionn to defeat his. And Patrick held this to be true, for he knew of that other Arthur in his own day.

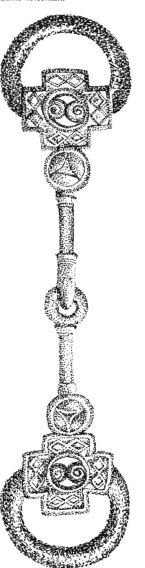

This flexible bridle bit found in London is an excellent example of the kind of equipment used by Celtic horseman.

The Hostel of the Quicken Trees

Most would agree that of all the warriors who served with Fionn mac Cumhail in the Fianna, Diarmuid O'Duibne was the greatest. No task for him was too great, no feat of arms or course of hunting too hard that he would not try it. And he had besides a face and form that women loved, which caused great sorrow among the Fianna in time to come. But while Diarmuid rode with them, they were the most unbeatable men in all of Ireland.

The coming of Diarmuid was this wise: as a boy he went with other boys to be trained by the great warrior-woman, Mongfinn, but in time he came to leave there, and, with his youthful companions, made for Allmu of the White Walls to take service with Fionn.

On the way they came to a ford in the river and by its banks was an old woman who begged them to carry her across. All of the boys refused, fearing

35

to dirty their immaculate clothes with the mud of the river. Only Diarmuid took pity on the old woman, and waded across the river with her in his arms. As he reached the other side, however, his companions having gone ahead without him, he found the old woman had become a great shining figure that he knew for one of the Lordly Ones out of Tir-nan-Og.

She smiled at him and said, 'Diarmuid O'Duibhne, you are a good son and will do many great deeds; and for the goodness you had to myself today I promise that no woman shall ever refuse you, nor be able to resist your look. And I tell you also that you have not seen the last of this place, for here shall be another feat attempted, that shall be remembered.'

And with these words there was suddenly no one there at all.

So Diarmuid went on to Allmu of the White Walls, and there Fionn saw him, and with his thumb of wisdom he knew what had occurred and that the old woman had been the Battle Goddess Morrighan, herself. But for her gift he felt troubled – doubts which were to prove well founded later on.

As to the prophecy that Diarmuid would come to that ford again, this is the way that it came about. Many years later, Fionn fought a battle against the King of Lochlan, and slew him and all his sons save one only – Midac, whom he took into his own house and afterwards gave lands on the coast of Ireland. But in all that time never a word of thanks was had from Midac, who continued in secret to plot against Fionn.

One day, it chanced that the Fianna were hunting in the hills to the west of Allmu, and as sometimes happened, Fionn and some of his men became separated from their fellows who were following the track of a boar towards Cnoc Fianna. As they went they saw a tall and handsome warrior coming towards them, and Fionn greeted him cheerfully enough when he saw that it was Midac. And the King of Lochlan's son smiled smoothly enough (though there were some among the Fianna who knew his true colour) and invited them to sup with him at the Hostel of the Quicken Trees, which was nearby.

To this Fionn agreed readily, and commanded that certain of the band, Oisin and Diarmuid, Fodla and Caoilte mac Ronan, and his own youngest son, Fiachna with his foster-brother Innsa, should remain behind until the remainder of the hunt came up with them. Then Fionn and Goll mac Morna, and Conan Maol and the rest, rode after Midac to the Hostel of the Quicken Trees.

It was a fair and beautiful building, with bright intricate carvings on the wood of its uprights, and a fresh thatch that shone in the sunlight like gold. And all around it grew quicken trees, with berries full and red upon them.

Fionn and his men followed Midac within and were amazed at the richness they beheld: fine hangings on every wall, soft couches to rest on, and a bright roaring fire in the hearth to warm them.

'Certainly you have done well by yourself,' said Fionn to Midac, but when he looked around their host was nowhere to be seen. 'Is this not a strange thing? And no servants to be seen either?' he asked.

'There is something stranger than that,' said Goll, 'For but a moment since the walls were hung with fine stuffs and now they seem but rough planks through which the wind blows.'

'And there is something else strange,' said Fiachna, 'When we came in there were seven doors but now there is only one, and that closed tight.'

'What is more,' added Conan, 'these soft couches we were sitting upon seem to have become as hard as the earth – perhaps because they are!'

Seeing treachery and magic thus revealed, the Fianna made to rise and break out of the hall – only to find that they could not move, but were anchored fast to the floor as though with bands of iron.

Then Fionn put his thumb of wisdom between his teeth and groaned aloud: 'Now is the treachery of Midac mac Lochlan revealed,' he said, 'for I see a great host coming against us, led by Sinsar of the Battles, and his son Borba the Haughty, and coming with them are the three sons of the King of Torrent. It is the last named whose spells hold us here and only the scattering of their blood on the floor will set us free. But of that there is little chance.'

Then the men of the Fianna sent up the war-cry, the Diord Fionn, and so loud was their cry that Fiachna and Innsa heard it and hurried down to the Hostel of the Quicken Trees to discover what was amiss. When they heard what had come to pass the two young warriors felt their battle-rage come upon them and they at once said they would defend the hostel at whatever cost – for there was a ford nearby that the enemy host must cross before they came where Fionn and his men were imprisoned.

Meanwhile, the host that was coming to destroy Fionn had made camp at a few miles' distance. It occured to one of Midac's chieftains that if he went with his own men and slew Fionn and brought the head back to his master, great fortune would be his. So he set off and came to the ford where Innsa and Fiachna waited. There ensued a great combat in which Innsa fell to Midac's chieftain, and Fiachna in turn slew him, along with so many of his warriors that only a handful returned to Midac.

Fiachna buried Innsa in a shallow grave and bore the news of his death and the slaughter of their enemies to Fionn, who wept for the death of his foster-son. But still he and the Fianna were held fast, nor would Fiachna abandon them and go for the rest of the warband.

Meanwhile, another chieftain of Midac's, named Ciaran, fell to wondering why his brother and their men had not returned, and set forth in search of them. When they came to the ford, they found it choked with the bodies of the slain, and Fiachna waiting to meet them.

Then there followed one of those combats that live in the memory of men long after. Fiachna held the ford alone against many dozens of attackers, and at the end of it only one man escaped to take the news to Midac.

He became so enraged that he gathered a part of his own men and made for the ford, where he found Fiachna still, leaning on his sword and bleeding from many wounds. When Midac saw all the bodies of his men where they made a wall of dead in the stream, he flung himself forwards and engaged the young hero in single combat.

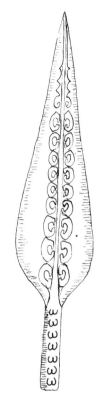

Spearheads (above and opposite) *discovered at Hiedersingen, near Stuttgart in West Germany. These magnificent examples of Celtic design are typical of the kind of weapons carried by the Fianna. The curvilinear designs are of bronze, cast into the blade.*

Meanwhile, Oisin, Fodla and Diarmuid had been waiting for word from Fiachna. When none came, Diarmuid and Fodla decided to go down to the Hostel of the Quicken Trees to find out what was amiss, while Oisin went after the rest of the warband. As they were nearing the place, they heard the sounds of battle and began to run, emerging at the place in time to see Fiachna, hard-pressed, give way before the fury of Midac's attack. Without pausing in his stride, Diarmuid flung his spear – a great throw which took Midac in the breast and laid him on his back – though not before he had struck once more a fatal blow that gave Fiachna his death.

Then, as Fodla gave battle to the rest of Midac's men, Diarmuid struck off the head of Fionn's enemy and carried it to the door of the Hostel. And when he found what had occurred there he groaned aloud, but said that he and Fodla would hold the ford against all comers until Oisin returned with the rest of the Fianna: 'And if the sons of the King of Torrent come hither while we wait, you may be sure you shall be set free the sooner.'

Diarmuid returned to the ford and found that Fodla had driven off the few remaining men of Midac's warband, and he was so exhausted with fighting that once he saw Diarmuid, he fell into a deep sleep there on the bank amid all the dead, and Diarmuid covered him with a cloak and left him to rest undisturbed.

Now, at last, the main body of the host that Midac had gathered, namely that of the three sons of the King of Torrent, came to the ford, and there for long hours Diarmuid held them at bay, single-handed, not liking to wake the sleeping Fodla. But in time the noise of the battle *did* awaken him and little pleased he was that he had missed so much of the fight.

The two warriors together drove back the enemy with dreadful slaughter, and in the end Diarmuid himself slew all three of the King's sons, and took their heads. Then while Fodla chased off the rest, Diarmuid went again to the Hostel of the Quicken Trees and sprinkled the blood on the doorstep and the earth within. But though Fionn and his men were able to move, they still had no strength, and Fionn told Diarmuid that they would not be able to fight before morning, when their strength would return.

So once again Diarmuid returned alone to the ford, and there he and Fodla awaited the last of their enemies: Sinsar of the Battles and his son Borba, with all their men.

This was the fourth combat of the Ford of the Quicken Trees, and it was a hard fight that continued all day and did not stop at sunset. But Diarmuid and Fodla, in a momentary lull in the fighting, spoke to each other and Diarmuid advised that they should hold off from attacking with equal ferocity to that of their enemies and save their strength until help arrived, or until Fionn could join with them.

In the early light of dawn came not only Sinsar and Borba, but also the King of the World with all his men; and then things might have gone ill indeed with Diarmuid and Fodla, but that with the first ray of the sun, Fionn and Goll and the rest received back all their old strength. Chanting their

38

battle cry, they joined in the fray. Things might still have gone ill for them, but before the morning was passed, Oisin and the rest of the Fianna came upon the scene. With all his warriors at his side, Fionn rose up in his battle fury and inflicted such slaughter that few men lived to speak of their defeat. Among the slain were both Sinsar and Borba, the sons of the King of the World. After that, it was a long time before any man of Ireland stood again against the Fianna. But it was only afterwards, when they rode away from the Hostel of the Quicken Trees, which they left in flames, that Diarmuid remembered the words of the Goddess he had carried on his shoulders long since, and then he knew that this was the same ford.

'And may it be a long while,' said Oisin to Patrick, 'before that fight is forgotten, nor the deeds of Diarmuid that day eclipsed by what came after.'

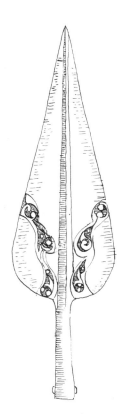

Diarmuid and Grainne

Now although Fionn served as chieftain of the Fianna at the behest of Cormac, the High King of Ireland, there came to be disquiet between the two of them, for in his heart Cormac feared the power of the Fianna, that they might some day look towards his throne and his kingship.

This grieved Fionn greatly, for he was a loyal man and hated there to be enmity between himself and the King. And it came to him that he should take a new wife, for he still thought of Sabha, Oisin's mother; and his second wife, Maighneis, had been dead for several years. So that Fionn grew lonely and when it was suggested that he ask for the hand of Cormac's daughter, Grainne, he was more than eager. He deemed that this was a way to heal the breach between himself and the High King, while at the same time gaining for himself a wife who was, by all accounts, the most beautiful in all of Ireland.

He duly sent messages to Cormac to ask for his daughter, and Cormac was not loath to give her up, for he too saw the chance to make a potential enemy a son-in-law. But as for Grainne herself, she was less willing. 'For,' she said, 'Fionn is no longer young, and there may yet come one whom I can truly love.'

But her father would not listen and commanded her to do as she was bidden, and to Fionn he sent back messages of friendship and acceptance of his offer.

So a great feast was prepared at Tara of the Kings, and folk came from all the five provinces of Ireland to grace the wedding of Fionn to Grainne. But on the night of the feast, Grainne sat silent and pale beside her new lord until she saw Diarmuid amongst the guests; and a blush of colour stole into her cheeks and she asked his name.

Then, taking the guest cup in her hands, Grainne moved among the throng speaking gently to one or laughing merrily with another, until she came to where Diarmuid sat and said softly, 'Diarmuid O'Duibhne, my heart is filled with love-longing for you.'

Diarmuid looked at the woman who had just become his lord's wife and for a moment his look answered her own, then he said that no man of Fionn's would ever betray him.

But Grainne said, simply, 'I lay this *geise* upon you, Diarmuid O'Duibhne, that you take me from this place tonight or leave this land as a man dishonoured.'

Then Diarmuid grew pale, for no warrior might refuse such a *geise*, yet he knew that once he left Tara with Grainne there would be no place for either of them beyond the reach of Fionn. But nonetheless he could not do otherwise, and as Fionn and all the Fianna, and the warriors of Cormac slept, Diarmuid O'Duibhne and Grainne, the daughter of the King, slipped out of Tara and fled away into the night.

Next day and for many days after they ran, for there would be no rest or respite from the pursuit of Fionn. Many times they heard the call of hounds, and more than once Diarmuid recognised either Bran or Sgeolan, but each time he managed to throw the scent.

So the days grew into weeks, and the weeks into months, and still the pair fled from the wrath of Fionn. Nowhere might they rest for more than a night, and to this day, right across Ireland are places known as the 'beds' of Diarmuid and Grainne, where they were believed to have slept. And if Diarmuid began with no heart for the venture, as day followed day in the company of Grainne, slowly the barrier melted and he began to love her in truth.

But Grainne grew very thin and brown and her once carefully dressed hair was wild as a cloud from which her face looked out great-eyed at the world. But she never flinched from the steepest path or the hardest road, and followed unhesitatingly wherever Diarmuid led.

Several times Aengus Og, who was the foster father of Diarmuid, rescued them when the Fianna were close upon their heels, so that never once in all that time did Fionn set eyes upon either one of them, though he followed for more than a year and a half. Until at last, Aengus Og himself went to Fionn and asked whether he would not give up the chase and let Diarmuid and Grainne live in peace. Fionn, who was growing old, shrugged and said that he would, so long as Diarmuid stayed away from Allmu. Then Aengus went in turn to Cormac and asked him the same thing. Though Cormac was in no way pleased that a man had taken his daughter when she had just become betrothed to a man of Fionn's standing, yet he agreed.

His son, Cairpre, was less willing, and became the greatest enemy of the Fianna from that time.

So Diarmuid and Grainne were allowed to settle down together on land that belonged to the O'Duibhne's, and Diarmuid had besides a gift of land from Fionn, as befitted a hero who had served him well. Thus, all went well

with them for a number of years, until Diarmuid had four sons to his name and had begun to lose some of his youthful beauty.

Then, one day, Grainne said to him: 'Is it not a shame that in all these years Fionn has never once visited us here, or that you have never ridden hunting with the Fianna on these lands?' Diarmuid, who in truth had missed his old comrades, roused himself to send word to Fionn that if he saw fit they should forget the enmity that had been between them and ride once more together.

So it was that in the spring of that year, Fionn and a small band of the Fianna came to Diarmuid's house and there was feasting and much talk of old battles and sport. And when Fionn proposed to hunt the lands around Ben Bulben, that lay within Diarmuid's lands, there was a gladness between them.

Now there was one beast that Diarmuid might never hunt because of a *geise* laid upon him long ago in his youth – and that was the boar, for it was said that in this way would he come by his death. Yet several times in the night, he awoke to the voice of hound, and, it seemed, the noise of a great pig. He would have risen from his bed had not Grainne held him fast in her arms and bade him await the dawn. But when the day came at last, he would wait no longer. He set out alone with only a single hound for company, in search of that voice he had heard in the night. And so he came to a place near the top of Ben Bulben, and there was Fionn, alone, awaiting him. The two men looked at each other a long while.

'Have you come to try and kill me, Fionn mac Cumhail?' said Diarmuid.

But Fionn only looked at him strangely and said, 'One of the hounds of the Fianna escaped into the night and we have been trying to catch him again, but there is a great boar at large on this mountain and it has already killed several

41

of our hounds. You should not be here, Diarmuid O'Duibhne, knowing of the prohibition upon you.'

Diarmuid shook his head, 'I shall not run away from any pig,' he said. 'I will wait here to see what comes.'

So Fionn went in search of his men while Diarmuid remained sitting in the early morning sun on Ben Bulben. Thus he was when he heard a great crashing in the bushes below him and there came in sight the largest and fiercest looking boar he had ever seen.

'Now here is my death,' said Diarmuid, looking at the beast's red eye. 'I shall see if I can overcome it.'

He drew his sword and went forward against the beast with only his hound at his side. She, poor beast, died in the boar's first rush, and in the second Diarmuid received his own death wound, though he slew the boar also. And so was another prophecy of himself fulfilled, that if ever he hunted a boar thus would he find his death.

Thus Fionn and the Fianna found him later that day, with still some life left in him, and Fionn stood over him and said, 'I am not sorry to find you thus, for you have done ill by me.'

'In the name of the friendship that was once between us and for the deeds I have done in your name,' gasped Diarmuid, 'I ask you to give me water from your hands.' For he knew that Fionn had a special power: if he gave succour to any man in this way, that man would be healed.

Fionn hesitated for a moment, and others of the Fianna who were at hand murmured that he should help Diarmuid, for the sake of the good he had done in past times. So Fionn went to a place where water bubbled up from the earth and gathered some in his cupped hands. But as he made to take it to Diarmuid, he remembered Grainne and the hurt he had been done, and allowed it to trickle out between his fingers. Then he took thought of the Hostel of the Quicken Trees and of other deeds of Diarmuid, and grew ashamed, so that he went for more water. But he was too late, for the life had gone from the hero before he could reach him.

Thus was the death of Diarmuid, and many of the Fianna mourned for him, as did Grainne, who dwelled alone for many years and taught her sons to hate Fionn. But in time her sorrow faded and with it her anger, and when Fionn called upon her to come back to Allmu of the White Walls as his wife, she did not refuse, but made peace between herself and his sons and the men of the Fianna.

The Death of Fionn

On a day in the summer of the year when Oisin came to stay at the monastery of Ard Macha, one of the monks came in haste to fetch Patrick with the news that 'Another devil is come, just like the other, but blacker.'

When he hastened to the bothy which was Oisin's, he found a great white horse, larger than any he had seen, tied up before it. Within he found Oisin deep in conversation with a great black-browed warrior who carried a sword big enough to need two ordinary men to lift it.

Oisin rose to his feet, his eyes shining as they had rarely done since his first meeting with the monks.

'There is a new story I would have you hear, Talkend,' he said, 'One that you may not hear from my lips, but which concerns the death of Fionn mac Cumhail and the ending of the Fianna. Will you hear it?' So Patrick sent for his scribe and sat down to listen to the black-browed stranger. This is the tale he told. . . .

Ben Bulben in Co. Sligo. The huge bulk of the mountains rises in a landscape where the Fianna often hunted and where the hero Diarmuid met his death.

The time came when Cormac mac Art died and his son, Cairpre, became High King of Ireland in his place. But Cairpre hated the Fianna just as Cormac had loved them, and he plotted daily to find ways to destroy Fionn and his companions.

Now Cairpre had a daughter named Sgeimh Solais, who had many suitors. When at length one was found who was deemed suitable, a great banquet was planned to celebrate the forthcoming nuptials.

It was customary at such times for the High King to award the Fianna twenty ingots of gold as an extra fee for keeping guard over Ireland, and for them to send their youngest member to collect this tribute. On this occasion, it fell to the lot of a youth named Ferdia to collect the gold. Though Fionn and his men waited all day outside the walls of Tara of the Kings, it was late before Ferdia returned. When he did, it was not as a living man but as a corpse, flung over the walls of Tara with these mocking words of Cairpre:

43

'Too often have the Fianna made demands of the High Kings of Tara. This is the only answer they will get from now on.'

Fionn strode out to the front of the Fianna and shouted up at the walls of Tara, 'Cairpre mac Cormac, you have earned your death by this action. When next we meet, look to yourself.'

Then he and all of the Fianna that were with him, turned away from Tara and returned to Allmu of the White Walls to prepare for war.

But there were those of the Fianna who would not fight against the High King, preferring either to remain neutral or to join the opposing army. Thus, in the end, Fionn had only the men of his own clan Bascna, and those of Leinster under the captaincy of Oscar son of Oisin, and the army of King Feircobh of Munster, who had married into Fionn's family and was a firm comrade besides. This was in all but 3,500 men.

But Cairpre had 3,000 warriors of Tara on his side, as well as the clan of Morna – for though Goll mac Morna remained true to Fionn, there were many among his own clan that remembered the old feud and who hated Fionn for ousting Goll from the captaincy of the Fianna. These were 2,000 men, led by Fear-Taigh and Fear-Ligh mac Morna, Goll's younger brothers. As well as these, Cairpre had 1,000 men each from the tribes of Ulster and Connacht. From the Men of the Snows, the Men of the Green Swords and the Men of the Lion, he also had 1,000, each company led by one of the five sons of Urgriu. In all, it was an army of 10,000 men that Fionn had to meet with his own small force. The place of meeting was at Gaohra which lay to the West of Tara.

It was a very hard battle, with terrible losses on either side. None there were who fought more bravely than Oscar, son of Oisin, so that men said it was his day. Five score of the Men of the Green Swords and seven score of the Men of the Lion alone he slew. And at the last he came face to face with the High King himself.

He cast his spear at Cairpre, which passed through his body and stuck out beyond. But Cairpre with his last breath struck Oscar a terrible blow which let out most of the life from him. Yet when he saw that Cairpre's men had set his helm upon a pillar so that it might seem that he lived yet, Oscar drew upon the last of his strength to fling a thin slab of stone which struck the helm and broke it in pieces. But his own heart broke at that moment and he fell dead.

Then Caoilte mac Ronan and Conan Maol lamented the death of the great Fenian, and together they lifted and carried him to where Fionn stood. There, amid the press of battle, Fionn gave a great cry of anguish and raised the Diord Fionn, the Cry of the Fianna. He spoke words above the body of Oscar, before he plunged again into the thick of the fighting, and men say that never in all the history of the Fianna were such deeds done as were done by Fionn mac Cumhail that day. A mighty man he was still, though his hair and beard were white as flax, and in his shining war-coat and helmet of gold he was a figure terrible to all his enemies.

Fear-Taigh and Fear-Ligh mac Morna he slew and many dozens of warriors from the men of Connacht and the men of Ulster and none might stand before him. But at the last he stood alone, with most of his fellows dead or sore wounded, and then there came around him the five sons of Urgriu, who had commanded the pillars of the High King's army. When Fionn saw them he let fall his shield, which was all hacked and hewn, and grasping his great sword in both hands he went to meet them. . . .

'Thus perished that day Fionn mac Cumhail, captain of the Fianna of Ireland, and with him fell the most of his captains and many of his men. The might of the Fianna was smashed in that battle, and never again rode to hunt upon Cnoc Fianna, or Ben Bulben, Slieve Cua or Slieve Crot.'

The stranger fell silent while Oisin wept for the death of Fionn and for his own son, Oscar. Even Patrick was not wholly dry-eyed, though his sternness forbade that he should weep for a pagan. And Oisin, seeing or sensing this, rose to his feet and made this lay:

I used to serve an army on a hill, Patrick of the closed-up mind; it is a pity you to be faulting me; there was never shame put on me till now.

I have heard music that was sweeter than your music, however much you are praising your clerks; the song of the blackbird of Leiter Laoi, and the sound of the Diord Fionn; the very sweet thrush of the Valley of the Shadow, or the sound of the boats striking the strand. The cry of the hounds was better to me than the noise of your schools, Patrick.

The twelve hounds that belonged to Fionn, the time they would be let loose facing out from the *Siuir*, their cry was sweeter than harps and than pipes.

I have a little story about Fionn; we were but fifteen men; we took the King of the Saxons of the feats, and we won a battle against the King of Greece.

We fought nine battles in Spain, and nine times twenty battles in Ireland: from Lochlann and from the eastern world there was a share of gold coming to Fionn.

My grief! I to be stopping after him, and without delight in games or in music; to be withering away after my comrades; my grief is to be living. I and the clerks of the Mass books are two that can never agree.

If Fionn and the Fianna were living, I would leave the clerks and the bells; I would followed the deer through the valleys, I would like to be close to his track.

When he was done he said: 'I will not stay here longer, Talkend; though you have been kind this is not my home. One has come for me who will take me back to where Niamh awaits me yet, and mayhap her magic can make me young again.'

Patrick looked at the strange warrior, who nodded. 'It is Caoilte mac Ronan who is under your roof. I have come for my old comrade to take him where the Fianna await his return.'

Then Patrick arose and blessed them both and bade them speed well. Nor was it without sorrow that he watched them ride away together on the back of the great white steed, for he had grown fond of the old warrior in the months that he had remained at Ard Macha. But as to the stories of the Fianna, those Patrick kept; and it is said that he collected others from men who still remembered the ancient times, so that the memory of the Fianna and their heroes should not die out in the world.

Hero List of the Fianna

'This is the enumeration [and description] of Finn's people: their strength was seven score and ten officers, each man of these having thrice nine warriors, every one bound (as was the way with Cuchullin in the time when he was there) to certain conditions of service, which were: that in satisfaction of their guarantee violated they must not accept material compensation; in the matter of valuables or of meat must not deny any; no single individual of them to fly before nine warriors.

Of such not a man was taken into the Fianna; nor admitted whether to the great Gathering of Usnach, to the Convention of *Taillte*, or to Tara's Feast; until both his paternal and his maternal correlatives, his *tuatha* and kindreds, had given securities for them to the effect that, though at the present instant they were slain, yet should no claim be urged in lieu of them: and this in order that to none other but to themselves alone they should look to avenge them. On the other hand: in case it were they that inflicted great mischiefs upon others, reprisals not to be made upon their several people.

Of all these again not a man was taken until he were a prime poet versed in the twelve books of poesy. No man was taken till in the ground a large hole had been made (such as to reach the fold of his belt) and he put into it with his shield and a forearm's length of a hazel stick. Then must nine warriors, having nine spears, with a ten furrows' width betwixt them and him, assail him and in concert let fly at him. If past that guard of his he were hurt then, he was not received into Fianship.

Not a man of them was taken till his hair had been interwoven into braids on him and he started at a run through Ireland's woods; while they, seeking to wound him, followed in his wake, there having been between him and them but one forest bough by way of interval at first. Should he be overtaken, he was wounded and not received into the Fianna after. If his weapons had quivered in his hand, he was not taken. Should a branch in the wood have disturbed anything of his hair out of its braiding, neither was he taken. If he had cracked a dry stick under his foot [as he ran] he was not accepted. Unless that [at his full speed] he had both jumped a stick level with his brown, and stooped to pass under one even with his knee, he was not taken. Also, unless without slackening his pace he could with his nail extract a thorn from his foot, he was not taken into Fianship: but if he performed all this he was of Finn's people.

A good man verily was he that had those Fianna, for he was the seventh king ruling Ireland: that is to say there were five kings of the provinces, and the king of Ireland; he being himself the seventh, conjointly with the king of all Ireland.

Finn's two poll-wards were Noenalach, and Raer grandson of Garb; the two stewards of his hounds: Crimthann and Connla Cas; his dispenser: Cathluan son of Crimthann; his master of the banquet: Corc son of Suan; his three cupbearers: Dermot grandson of Duibhne, and Faillin, and Colla son of Caeilte; the two overseers of his hearth; Caeilte and Glanna; his two makers of the bed; Admoll and mac Neri; his twelve musicians: Fergus True-mouth, Fianu, Bran, two Reidhes, Nuada, and Aithirne Aghmar, and. . . . Flann and Aedh, Cobthach of the high strains, and Cethern; his physician: Lerthuile; his two keepers of the vessels: Braen and Cellach Mael; his barber: Scannal; his comber: Daelgus; his charioteer: Rinnchu; his two masters of the horse: Aena and Becan; his strong man: Urchraide grandson of Bregaide; his six door-keepers: Cuchaire and Bresal Borr, Fianchad and *Mac-dá-fer*, Imchad and Aithech son of Aithech-bal; his carpenter: Donngus; his smith: Collan; his worker in metal: Congaran; his horn-players: Culaing and Cuchuailgne; his two soothsayers: Dirinn and Mac-reith; his carver: Cuinnscleo; his candle-holder: Cudam; his two spear-bearers: . . . and Uadgarb; his shield-bearer: Railbhe, and so on.

(The Enumeration of Finn's People
trans: Standish O'Grady)

Fionn's Battles

This list of some of Fionn's greatest battles comes from an ancient Irish poem describing his shield, the history of which is then given, including details of the great battles in which it was carried:

What of battles were fought by thee under Cumhall's son of the bright hands, thou brightest shield that hast not been defamed, 'twere hard to number them.

By thee was given the battle of Ceann Cluig, when Dubhthach, son of Dubh, was slain: the battle of Móin Mafaidh without woe, when Déidgheal hard-mouth was slain.

The battle of Luachair, the battle of Ceann Aise, and the battle of Inbhear Dubhghlaise, the battle of Teathbha, stiff was its entanglement, the battle of Cluain Meann of Muirisg.

The battle of Lusga, the battle of Ceann Cláire, and the battle of Dún Maighe, the battle of Sliabh Fuaid, whose heat was tense, the rout in which fell rough grey-eyed Garbhán.

The battle of Fionntráigh, whereby the warsprite was sated, where blood and booty were left behind, two bloody battles round Ath Móna, and eke the battle of Cronnmhóin.

The battle of Bolgraighe of great deeds, in which fell Cormac the exact, the battle of Achad Abhla that was not slack, the battle of Gabhair, the battle of the Sheaves.

The battle of Ollarbha, where the strife was fierce, wherein generous Fathadh was slain, the battle of Eise, great were its deeds, and the battle of Ceis Corainn.

The battle of Carraig, the battle of Srubh Brain, and the battle of Beann Eadair, the battle of Sliabh Uighe that was not slack, and the battle of Magh Málann.

The battle of the brave Colamhnaigh, and the battle of

Inbhear Bádhna, the battle of Ath Modhairn, clear to us, and the battle of Beirge above Boyne.

The battle of Magh Adhair not belittled, and the battle of Dún Fraochán, the battle of Meilge of the mighty struggle, that caused loud cries and wails of woe.

The battle of Beirbhe, great was its deed, the after-battle with the King of Lochlainn of the ships, the battle of Uighe, undoubtful were its tidings, and the battle of the Isle of Gaibiel.

The battle of Móin, the battle of Ceann Tíre, and the fortunate battle of Islay; the battle of the Saxons, great was its glory, and the battle of sturdy Dún Binne.

The battle where tall Aichil was slain, the ready-handed high-king of Denmark, the battle of Inbhear Buille in truth, and the battle of fierce firm Buinne.

Twenty battles and twelve outside of Ireland in full sooth as far as Tír na n-Dionn of fame not small, Fionn fought of battles with thee.

Eight battles in Leinster of the blades thou and thy side-slender lord fought: in thy space of grace, no falsehood is this, sixteen battles in Ulster.

Thirty battles without reproach thou gavest in Munster of MacCon – it is no lie but sooth – and twelve battles in Connacht.

Twenty-five victorious battles were fought by thee, thou hardy door, eighteen battles, a rout that was not slack, thou didst gain over the Tuatha De Danann.

Not reckoning thy fierce indoor fights and thy duels of hard swords, these while thy success lasted strong were thy share of the battles of Ireland.

(trans: Eoin MacNeill)

Further Reading

Bruford, A. *Gaelic Folk Tales and Medieval Romance* Dublin, Folklore of Ireland Soc., 1969

Campbell, J. G. *The Fians*, D. Nutt, 1891

Cross, T. P. and Slover, C. H. *Ancient Irish Tales* Figgis, 1936

Cunliffe, B. *The Celtic World*, Bodley Head, 1985

De Breffny, B. (ed) *The Irish World*, Thames & Hudson, 1977

Delaney, F. *The Celts*, Hodder & Stoughton, 1986

Dillon, M. & Chadwick, N. *The Celtic Realms*, Weidenfeld, 1967

Dillon, M. *Cycles of the Kings*, Oxford Univ. Press, 1946

Gregory, Lady A. *Gods and Fighting Men*, Colin Smythe, 1970

Joyce, P. W. *A Social History of Ancient Ireland* (2 vols.), Longman, 1903

Kruta, V. *The Celts of the West*, Orbis, 1985

Laing, L. *The Archaeology of Late Celtic Britain and Ireland* Methuen, 1975

Lindsay, J. *Our Celtic Heritage*, Weidenfeld, 1971

Macalister, R. A. S. *The Archaeology of Ireland* Blom Inc., 1972

Maccana, P. *Celtic Mythology*, Hamlyn, 1970

McCone, K. R. 'Werewolves, Cyclops, Diberga and Fianna: Juvenile Delinquency in Early Ireland' in *Cambridge Medieval Celtic Studies* No. 12, pp 1–22, 1987

McMahon, A. (ed) *The Celtic Way of Life* O'Brien Press, 1976

MacNeill, E. & Murphy, G. *Duanaire Finn (The Book of the Lays of Fionn)* Dublin, Irish Texts Soc. (3 vols) 1908–53

Macpherson, J. *The Poems of Ossian* Patrick Gedds, 1846

Mageoghagan, C. *Annals of Clonmacnoise* London, 1627

Meek, D. R. 'The Banners of the Fian in Gaelic Ballad Tradition' in *Cambridge Medieval Celtic Studies* No. 11, pp 29–69, 1986

Meyer, K. (ed. & trans) *Fianaigecht* Hodges, Figgis, 1910

Morris, J. *The Age of Arthur*, Weidenfeld, 1973

Murphy, G. *Ossianic Lore*, Mercier Press, 1955

Newark, T. *Celtic Warriors*, Blandford Press, 1986

Nutt, A. *Ossian and the Ossianic Literature*, D. Nutt, 1899

O'Grady, S. H. *Fionn and his Companions*, Talbot Press, 1970

O'Grady, S. H. (ed. & trans.) *Silva Gadelica* (2 vols), Williams and Norgate, 1892

O'Rahilly, T. *Early Irish History and Mythology*, Dublin Institute for Advanced Studies, 1946

O'Riordan, S. P. *Antiquities of the Irish Countryside*, Methuen, 1965

Rolleston, T. W. *The High Deeds of Finn*, Harrap, 1910

Ross, A. *The Pagan Celts*, Batsford, 1986

Russel, V. *Heroes of the Dawn*, Maunsel, 1913

Scott, R. D. *The Thumb of Knowledge*, Institute of French Studies, 1930

Sutcliff, R. *The High Deeds of Finn mac Cool*, Bodley Head, 1967

Illustrations

Colour plates by James Field.
Line illustrations by Chesca Potter.
Map and diagram by Chartwell Illustrators.
Photographs courtesy of the Irish Tourist Board (pages 9, 25, 27, and 43), Northern Irish Tourist Board (page 7) and Trinity College Library, Dublin (page 13).

Index

Page numbers in *italics* refer to illustrations.